# MEXICAN MAFIA WEDDING

## TEHACHAPI PRISON 1978

Eric "Superman" Sturgess

Rose Of Sharon
PUBLISHING



ERIC "SUPERMAN" STURGESS

Printed Worldwide
First Printing 2025
First Edition 2025

10 9 8 7 6 5 4 3 2 1

Rose of Sharon Publishing books may be ordered through booksellers or by contacting:

Rose Of Sharon Publishing
roseofsharonpublishing.com
P.O. Box 186
Floresville, Texas 78114



ISBN: 978-1-970335-00-2 Paperback

# Dedication

Growing up in the 1970s and 1980s, Polaroid pictures were a common sight. I was always fascinated by them and how the picture slowly appeared over time. People would swing the photo back and forth like a hand fan to supposedly make the image appear quicker.

I have been collecting Polaroid pictures of convicts in the California Department of Corrections and Rehabilitation for several years now. They are rare and hard to find after all these years. The 1990s were the last decade when Polaroid pictures were commonly used in California state prisons.

These photos are a snapshot of time that captures these men doing their best to survive behind those cold prison walls. These photos and the people in them deserve to be seen by others and their lives not forgotten in the dustbins of history. It just reminds us how fleeting our lives are. Nobody is guaranteed tomorrow, and our youth quickly fades to old age if we are blessed to live that long.

God bless you
Eric Sturgess
Romans 10:9-13

# Preface

These Polaroid photos feature the wedding of Mexican Mafia member Danny "Dangerous Dan" DeAvila (CDC# B91609 from the Avenues) at Tehachapi State Prison on July 9, 1978. Robert "Robot" Salas (CDC# A83892 from Big Hazard), another La EME member, was his best man at his wedding, pictured. Manuel "Tati" Torres (CDC# A74921 from La Rana), another member of the Mexican Mafia, and his wife are also pictured at this wedding at Tehachapi Prison, sitting next to Dangerous Dan and his wife, with the wedding cake on the table in front of them.

Dangerous Dan was murdered at the Los Angeles County Jail on June 12, 1986. He was stabbed numerous times, and he died on the tier in a pool of blood in front of several prison cells. Word on the street is that he had fallen out of favor with his comrades, so they placed a green light on him.

All of the pictures in this book were taken during visits at Tehachapi State Prison. Inmates in the state of California are allowed to get married in prison. During this time, prisoners in the California Department of Corrections were allowed to wear their personal clothes to visits.

I came across these photos for sale on one of those auction sites one day. I thought the price was too high for what they appeared to be. I kept looking at them, and I realized that it was Robert "Robot" Salas pictured in one of them. I bought them, and when they arrived, the back of many of the photos contained names, dates, and other identifying information.

God bless you<br>
Eric Sturgess<br>
Romans 10:9-13

# Table of Contents

# Introduction

Some stories are written in ink, some are passed down in whispers, but the rarest are captured in fading Polaroid photographs. The pictures you hold in this book are more than images; they are pieces of history salvaged from one of the darkest and most secretive chapters of California's prison system.

On July 9, 1978, a wedding took place at Tehachapi State Prison. To the outside world, it was an ordinary summer day, but behind the cold prison walls, one of the Mexican Mafia's most infamous members, Danny "Dangerous Dan" DeAvila, said, "I do." At his side stood Robert "Robot" Salas, serving as best man, and Manuel "Tati" Torres, seated with his wife near the bride and groom. These men were not ordinary groomsmen and guests—they were legends within the Mexican Mafia, a brotherhood feared in every prison yard and barrio in California.

The Polaroids from that day show smiles, suits, and even a wedding cake—fleeting snapshots of everyday life in a place designed to strip men of it. They reveal how, even inside steel cages, convicts clung to the rituals of family, loyalty, and tradition. Yet they also expose a paradox: behind the laughter sat men who lived under a code of violence, where politics were deadly and betrayal carried a price that could only be paid in blood.

This is more than just a wedding album. Within a decade of the celebration, Dangerous Dan would be marked for death by his own comrades, hunted by men he once called brothers.

On June 12, 1986, in the Los Angeles County Jail, he was stabbed repeatedly until his breath left him on the bloodstained concrete floor. He chose to meet his fate head-on, going out the way prison culture defines a soldier. The very faces captured here in moments of celebration were bound by a world where alliances could collapse overnight, where envy, power, and politics could turn joy into a death sentence.

Every photo in this collection carries weight. Each image is a fragment of a story that history books will never tell. These are not Hollywood actors or fabricated legends; these were real men whose decisions and reputations shaped the culture of prison life across California for decades.

What you hold now is more than a photo book—it is a testimony. These Polaroids survived decades when most evidence of prison life was destroyed, hidden, or forgotten. They survived transfers, deaths, and the passage of time. To collectors, researchers, and those fascinated by the realities of organized crime and prison culture, they are priceless. They are a window into a world that few outsiders ever glimpse, and even fewer survive.
This book is for those who want to see beyond the stereotypes and myths. It is for those who understand that history is not clean—it is messy, brutal, and human. These men were fathers, husbands, and comrades. They laughed, they loved, they betrayed, and they bled. Their stories echo in these Polaroids, waiting for the reader willing to look closer.
As you turn each page, you step into a world of survival and politics, where fleeting joy is found in the shadow of inevitable violence. This is not just about Dangerous Dan or his wedding day. This is about a time, a culture, and the stark reality of prison life in California during the late 1970s and 1980s.

Look closely. Every face tells a story. Every photo is a reminder that history lives not only in official records but also in the quiet click of a Polaroid camera.

# Photographs

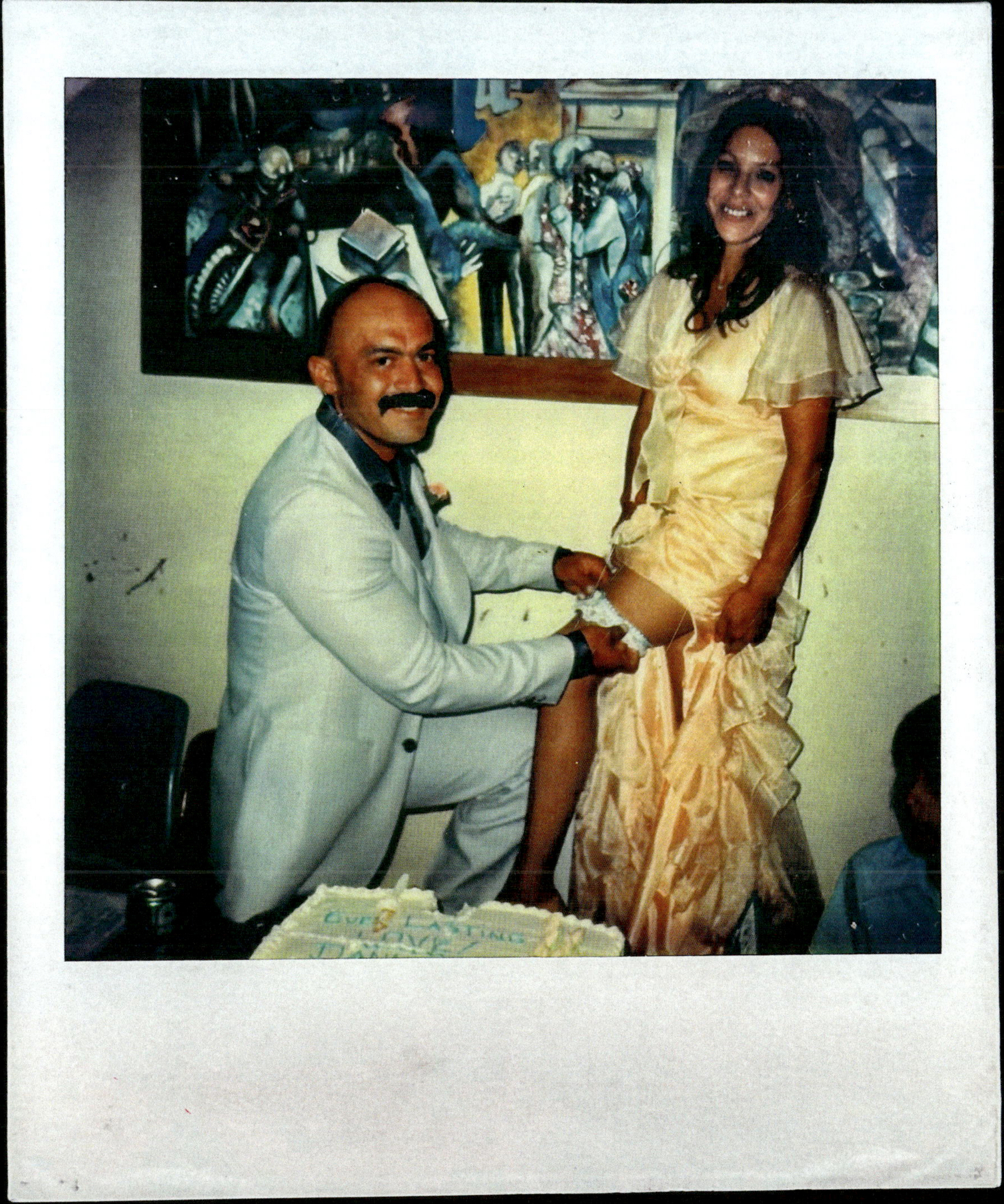

Danny "Dangerous Dan" DeAvila's wedding day at Tehachapi Prison on July 9, 1978.

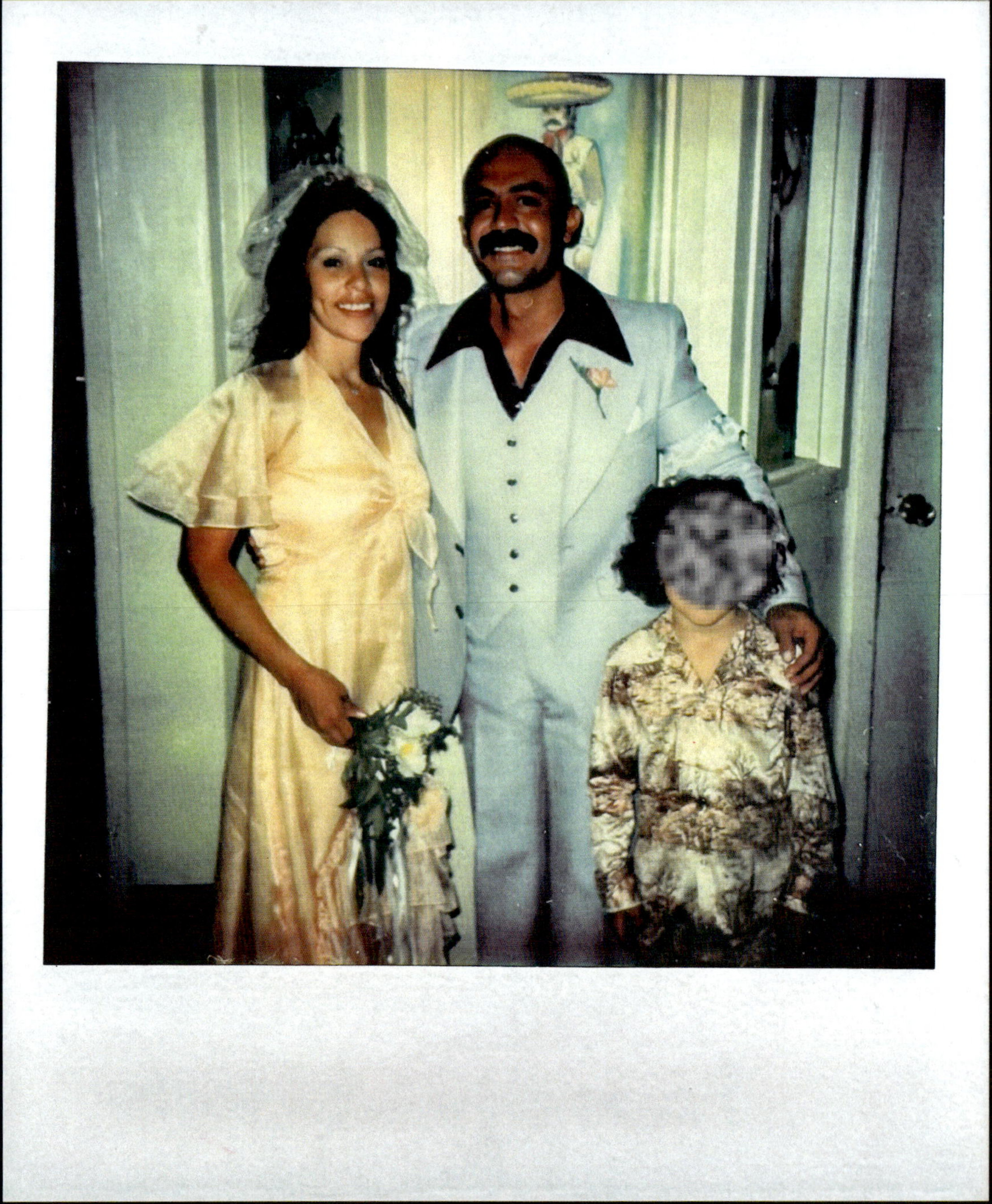

Danny "Dangerous Dan" DeAvila's wedding day at Tehachapi Prison on July 9, 1978.

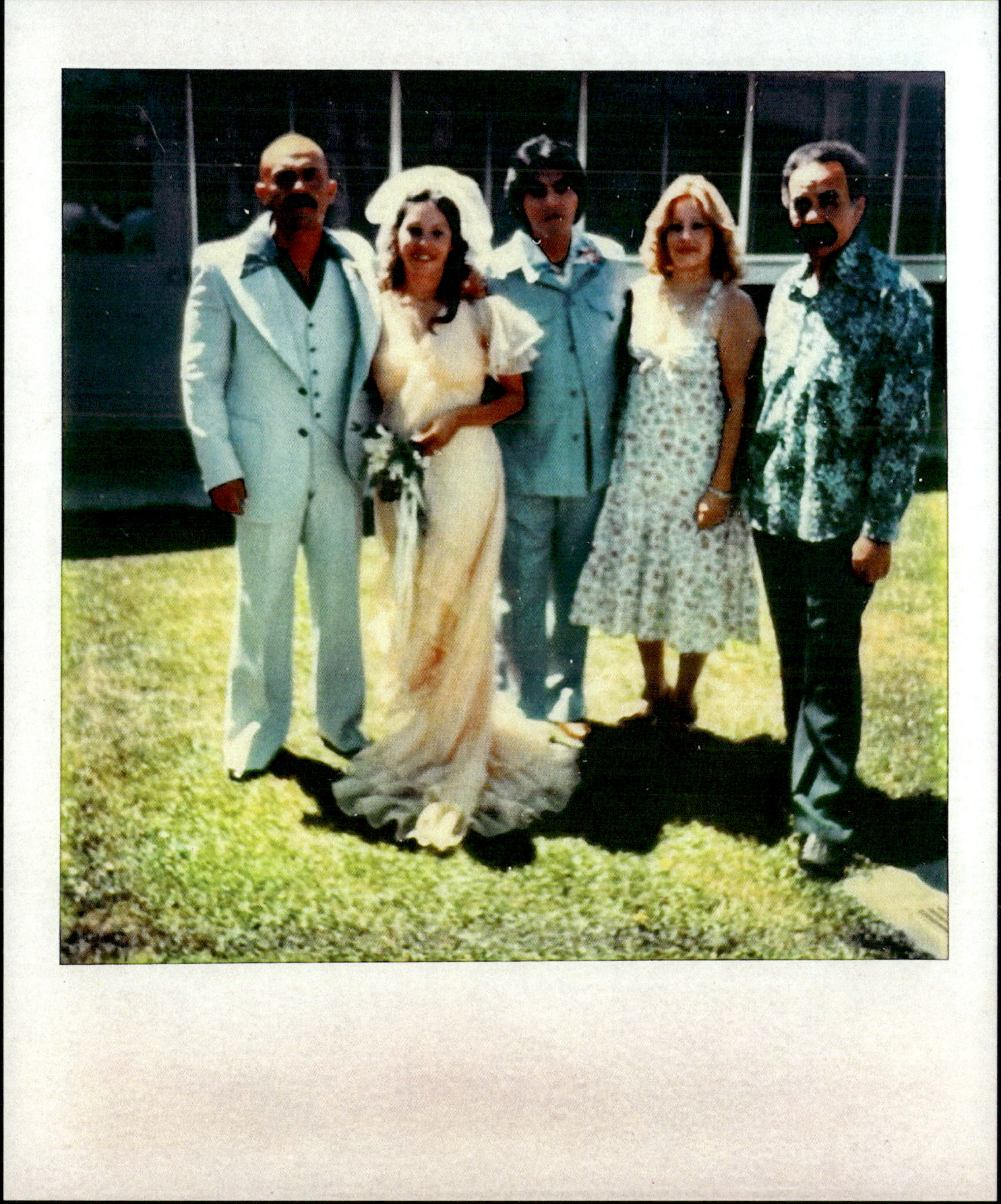

The best man at Dangerous Dan's wedding was Robert "Robot" Salas, a member of the Mexican Mafia, pictured here. This photo was taken at Tehachapi Prison on July 9, 1978.

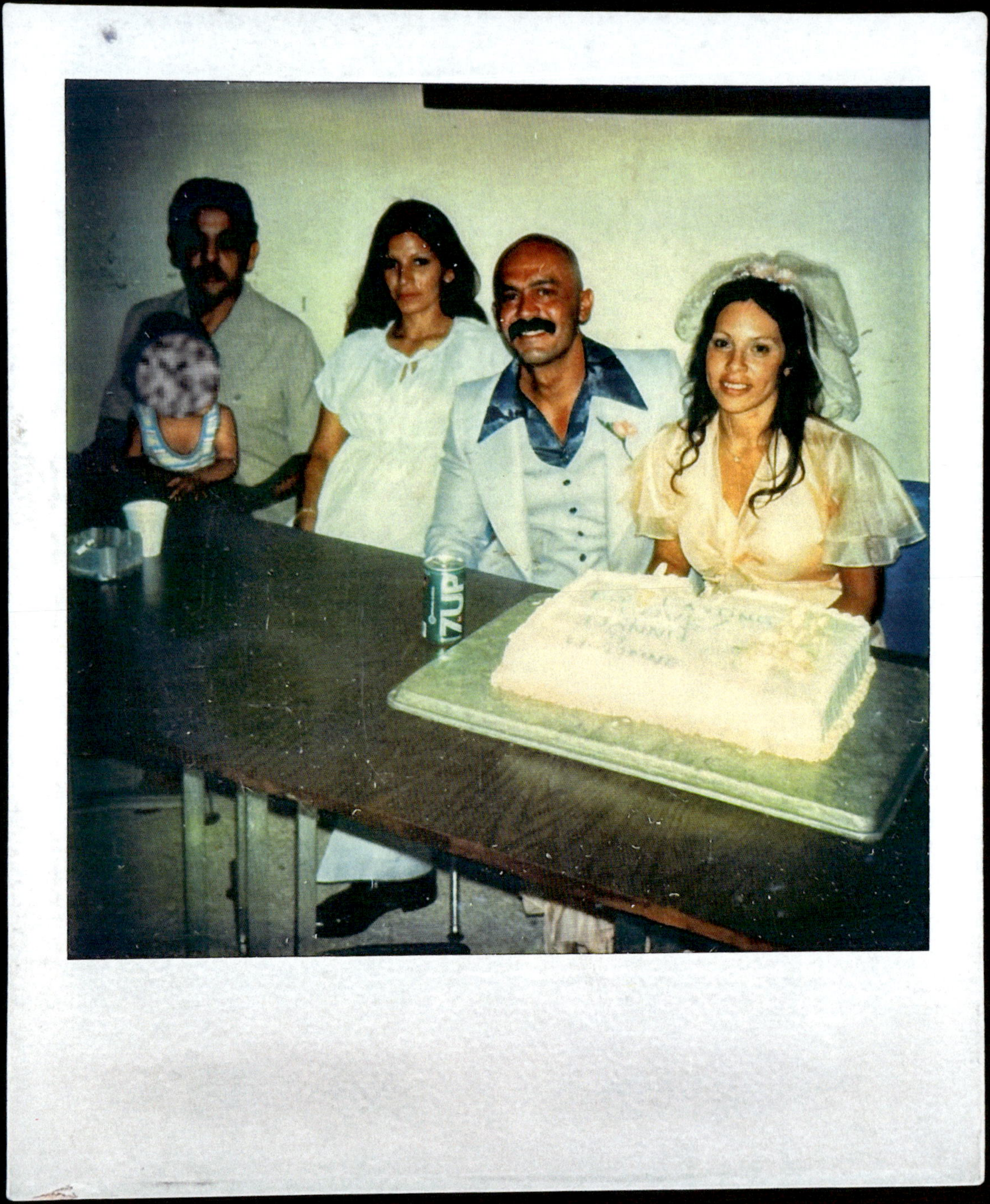


Dangerous Dan with his wife and Manuel "Tati" Torres and his wife. Tati was a highly influential member of the Mexican Mafia for many years. This picture was taken on July 9, 1978.

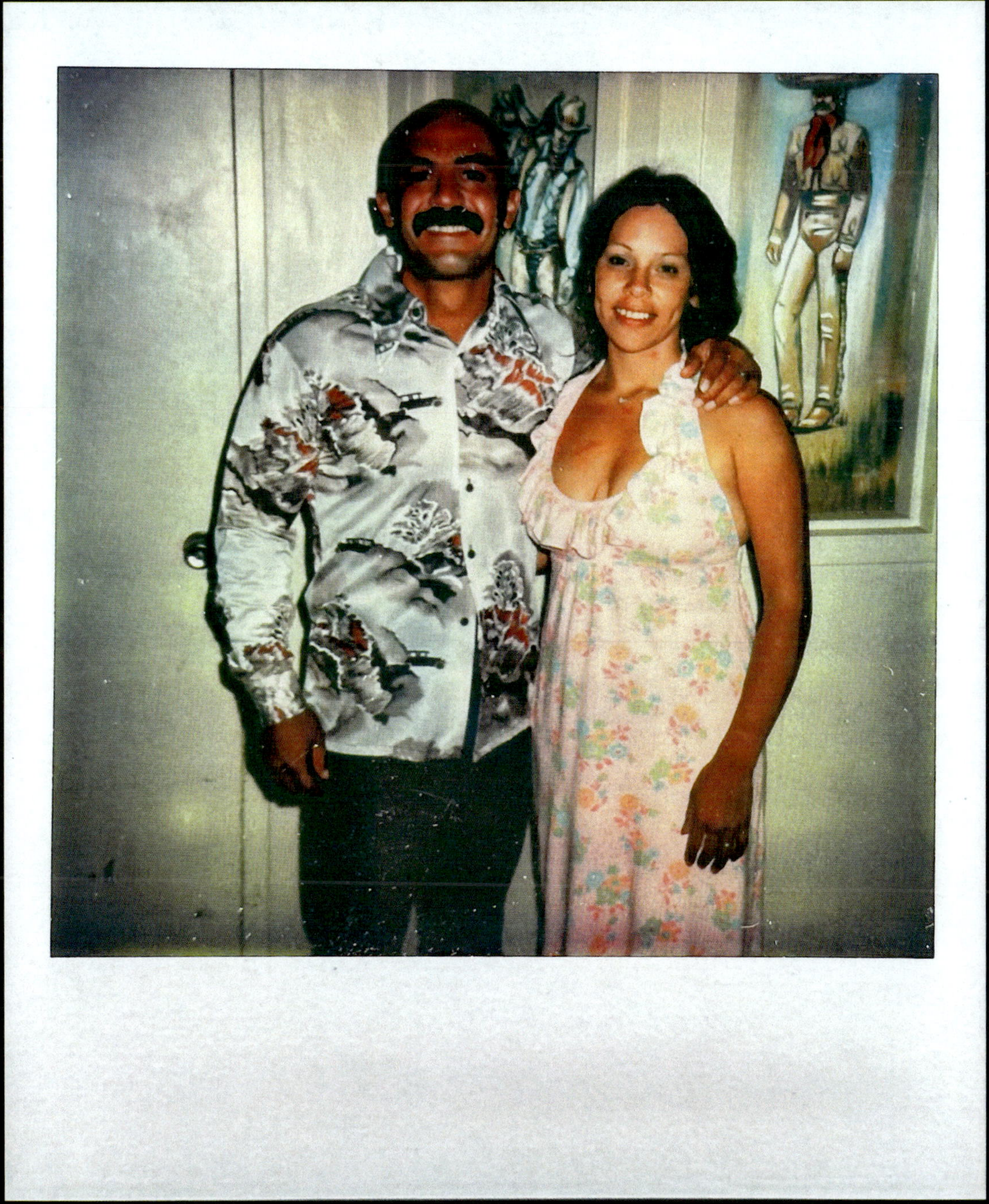

This photo was taken on July 5, 1978 at Tehachapi Prison during a visit.

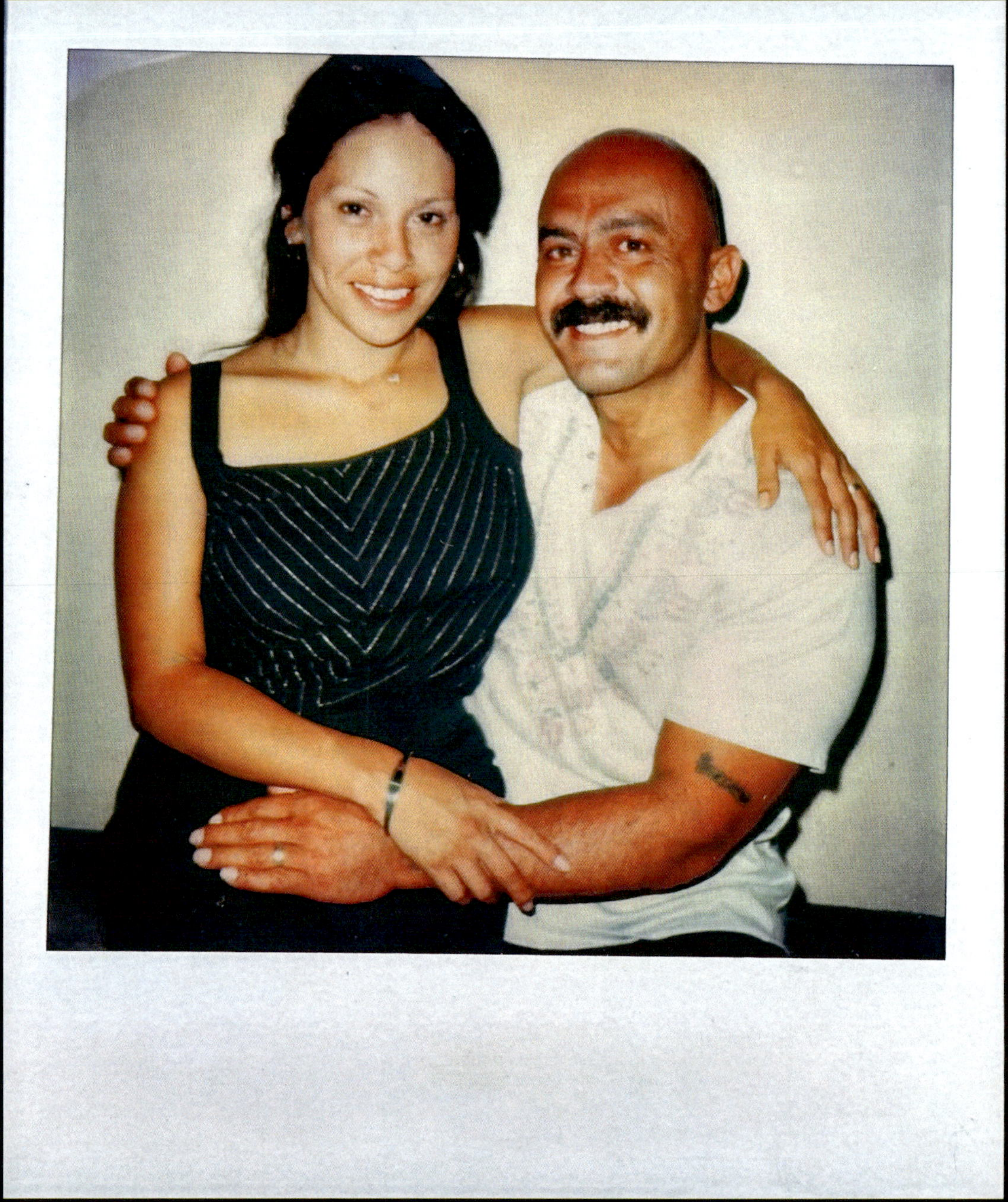

This photo was taken on July 4, 1978 at Tehachapi Prison during a visit.

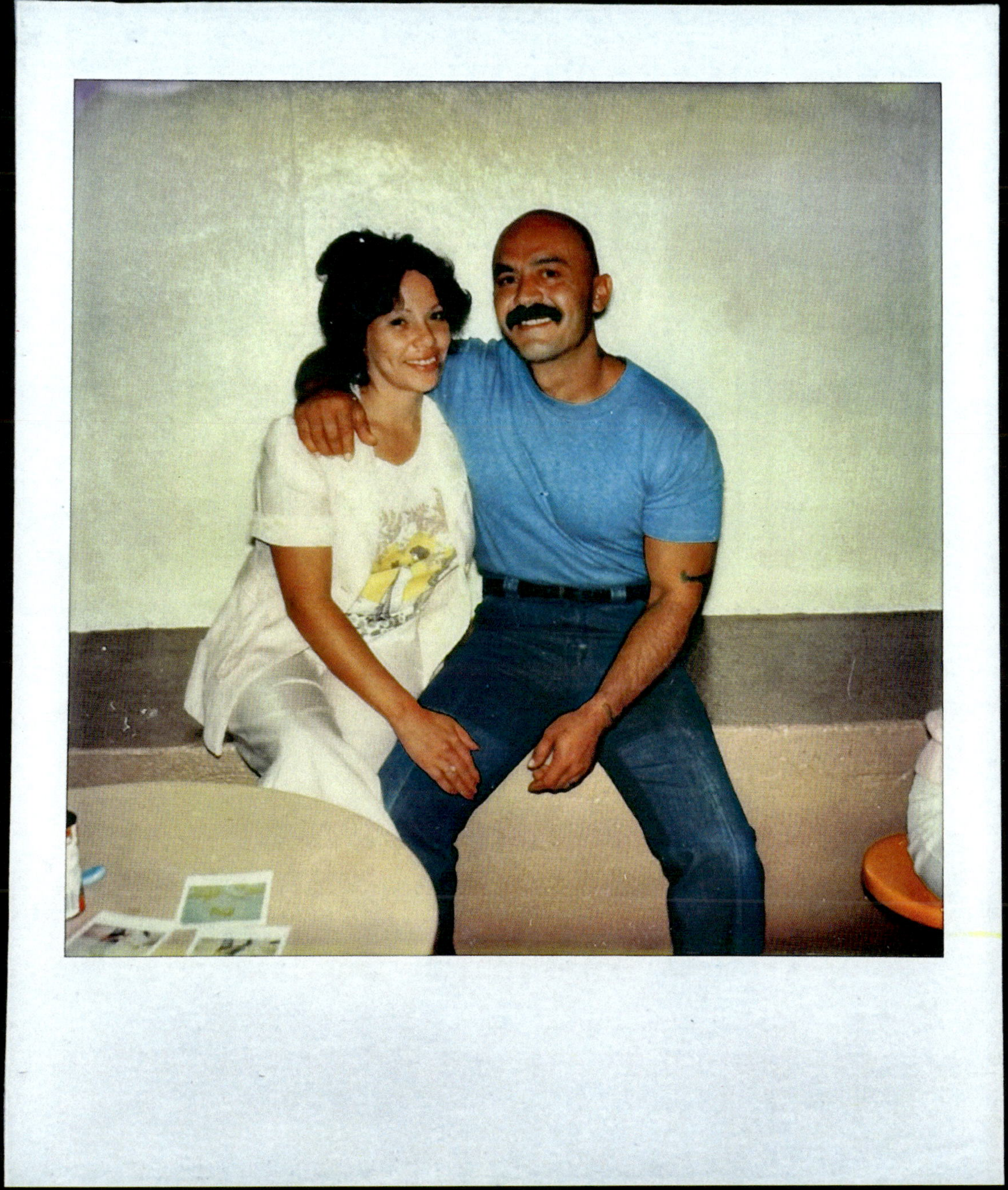

This photo was taken at Tehachapi Prison during a visit.

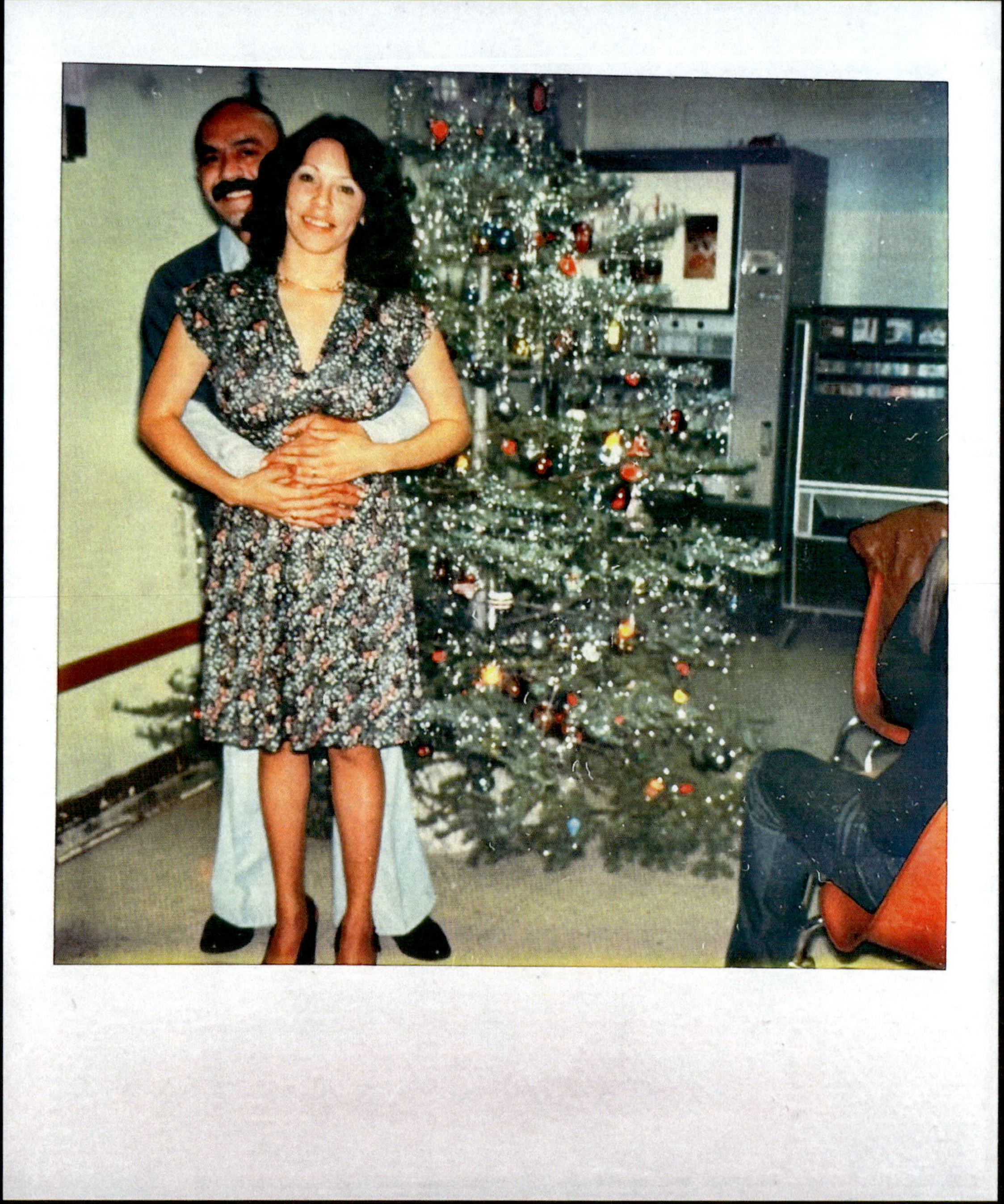

This photo was taken on December 19, 1978 at Tehachapi Prison during a visit.

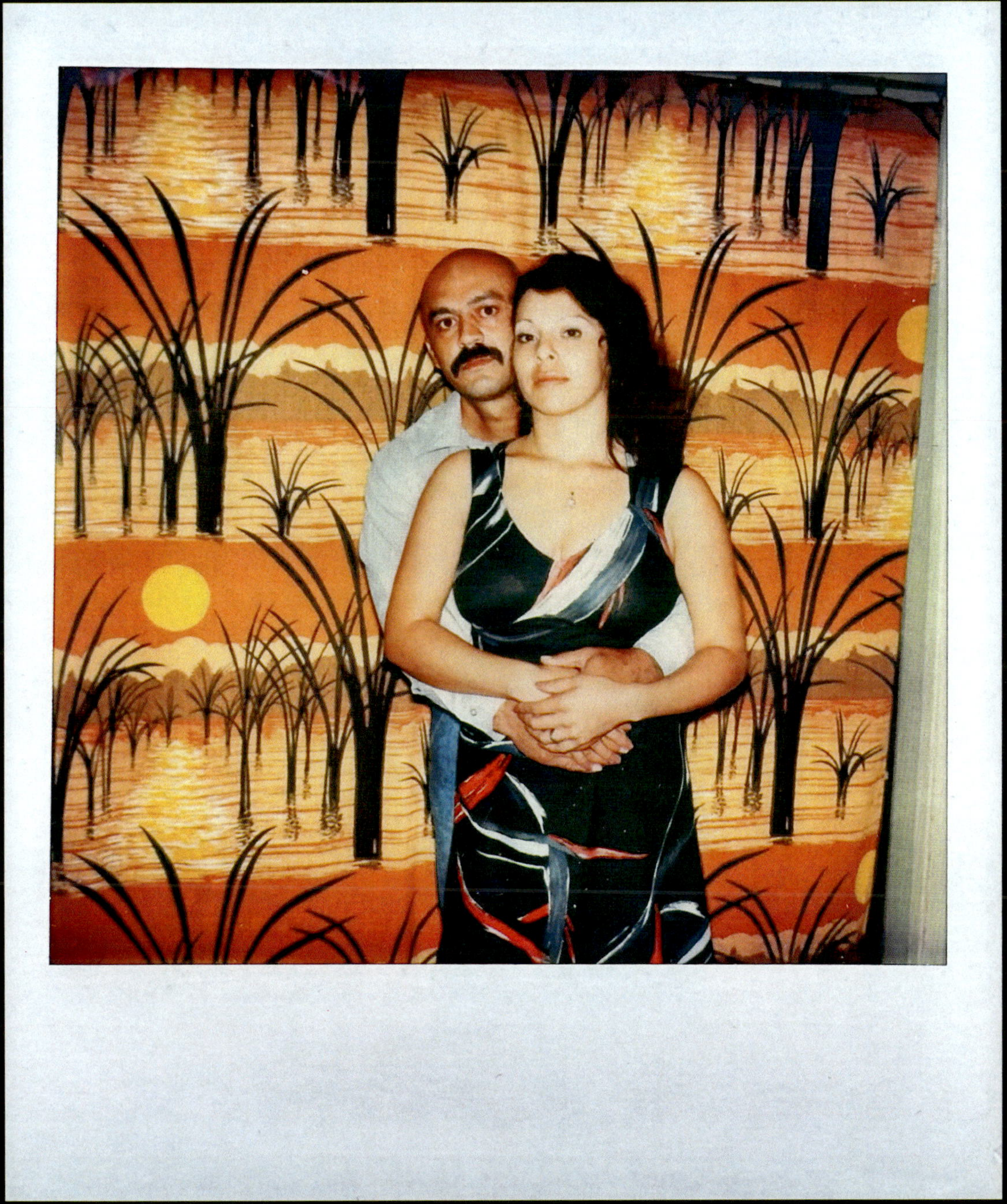

This photo was taken on November 21, 1978 at Tehachapi Prison during a visit.

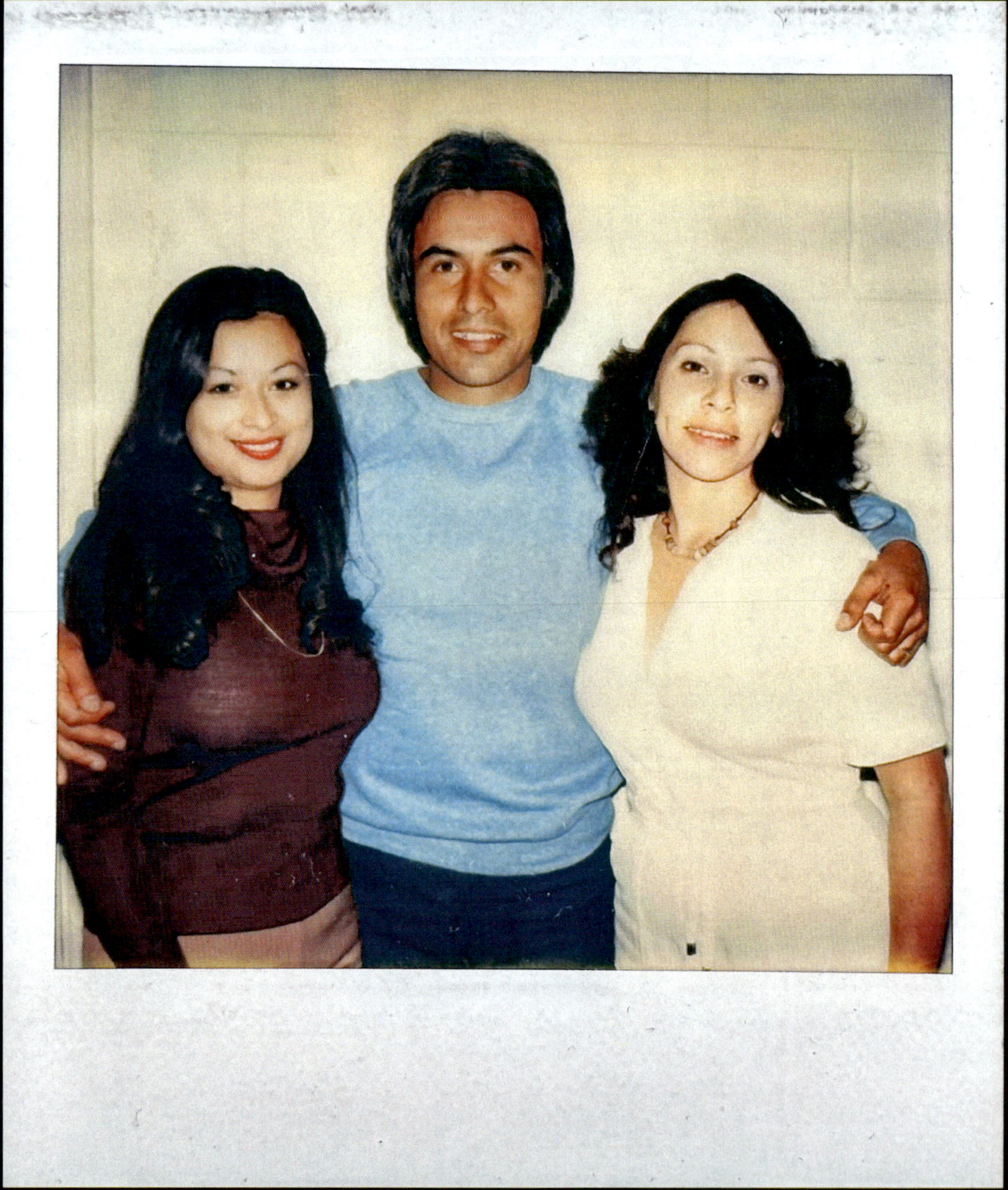

Robert "Robot" Salas is pictured with his wife on the left and Dangerous Dan's wife on the right. This photo was taken during a visit at Tehachapi Prison on December 16, 1978.

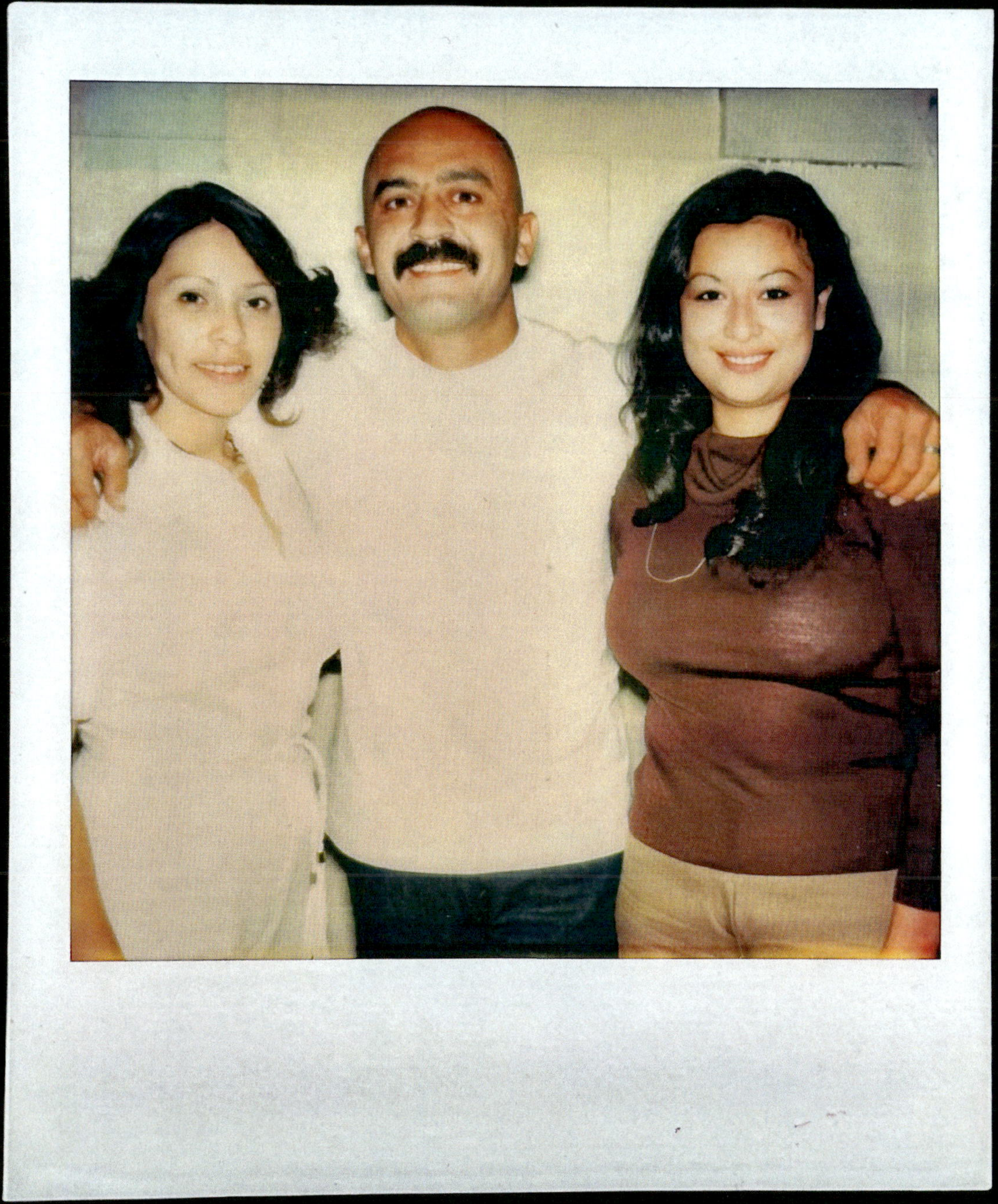

Dangerous Dan with his wife on the left and Robot's wife on the right. This photo was taken during a visit at Tehachapi Prison on December 16, 1978.

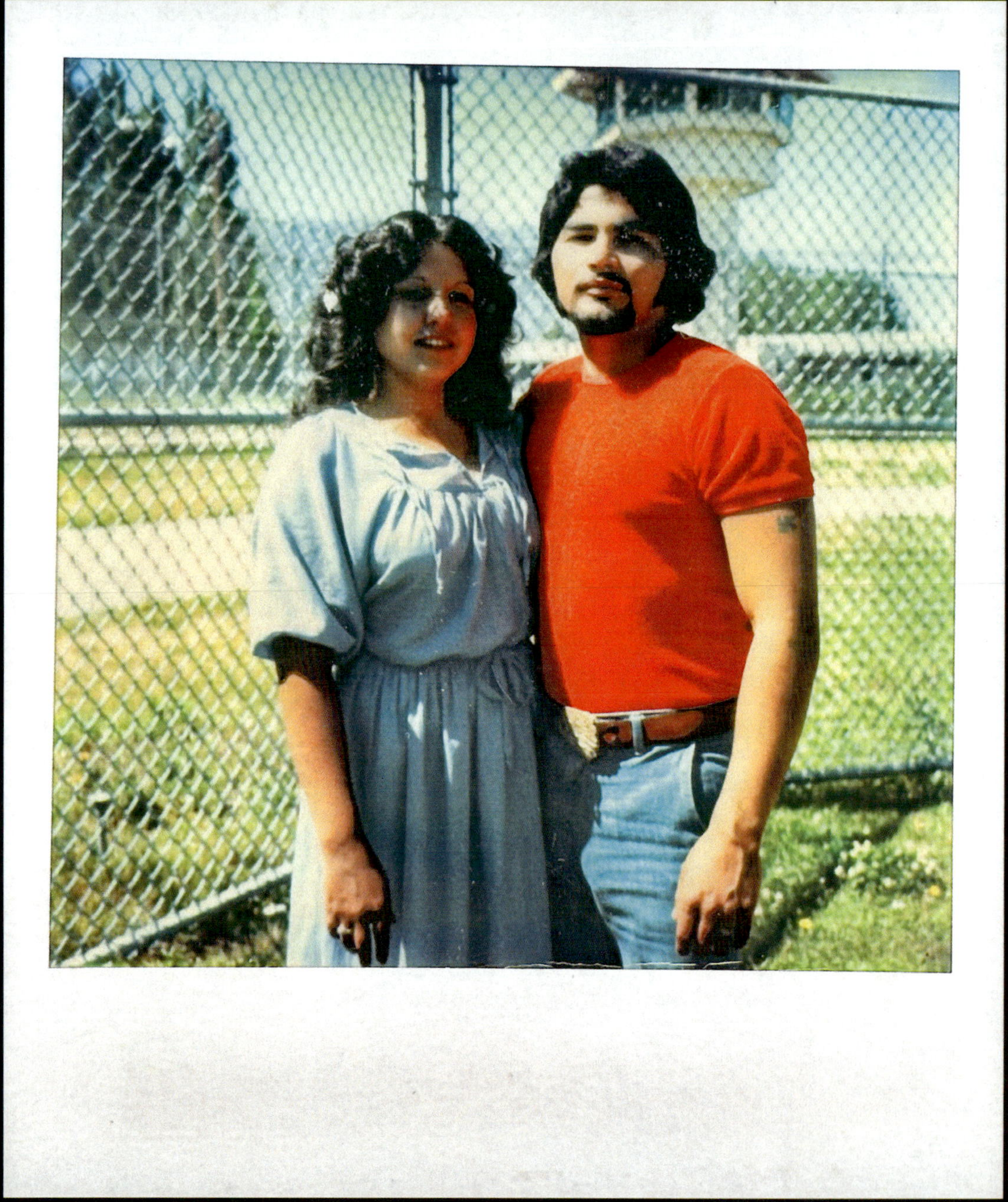

Thomas "Killer" Martinez, a Mexican Mafia member, is pictured here during a visit at Tehachapi Prison on June 11, 1978. He is from a Hispanic gang in Los Angeles called Dogtown, and they actually use a swastika as a symbol. That is why he has a swastika tattoo on his left arm. This photo was part of Dangerous Dan DeAvila's collection.

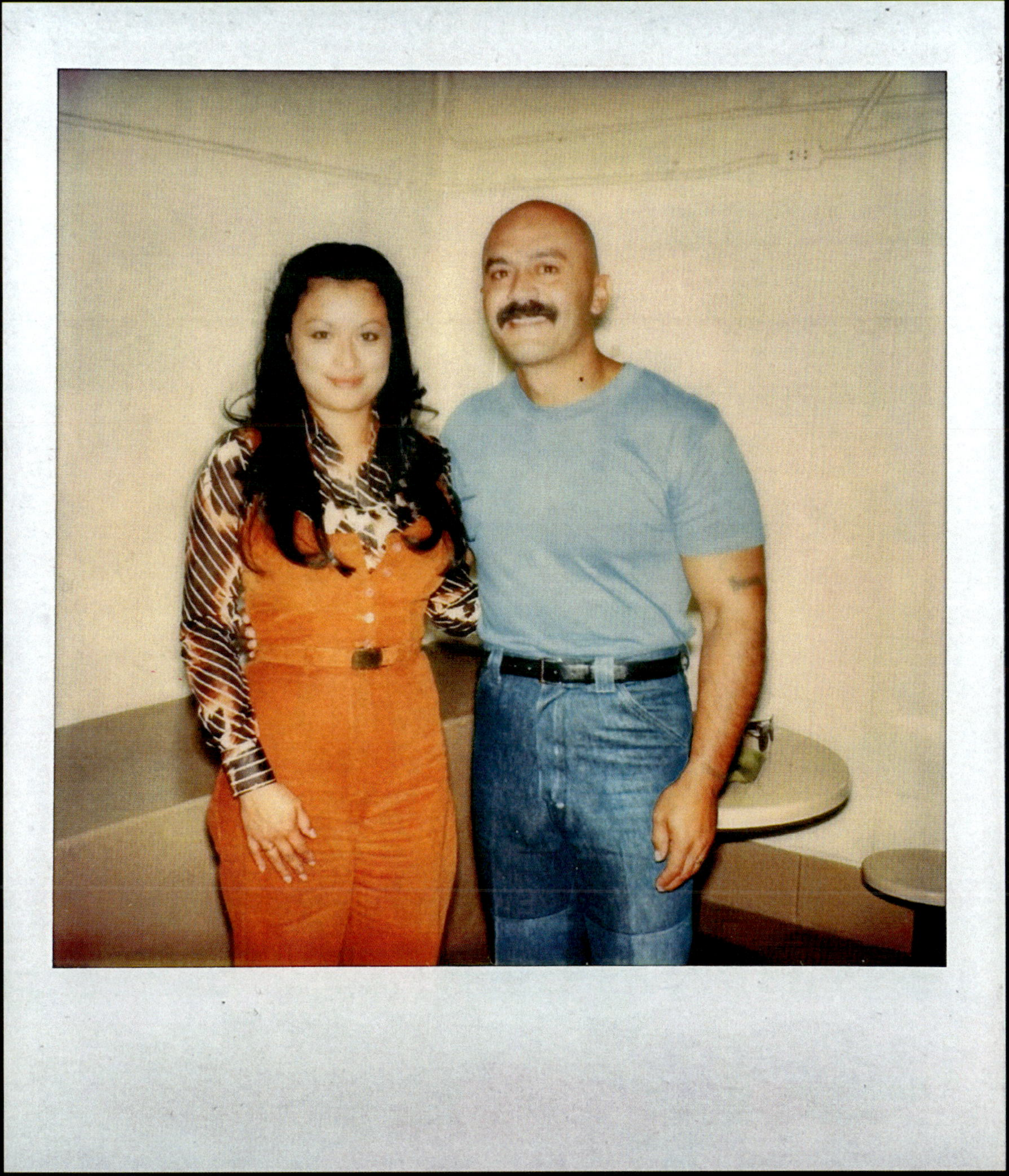

Dangerous Dan during a visit at Tehachapi Prison with the wife of Robert "Robot" Salas
on November 4, 1978.

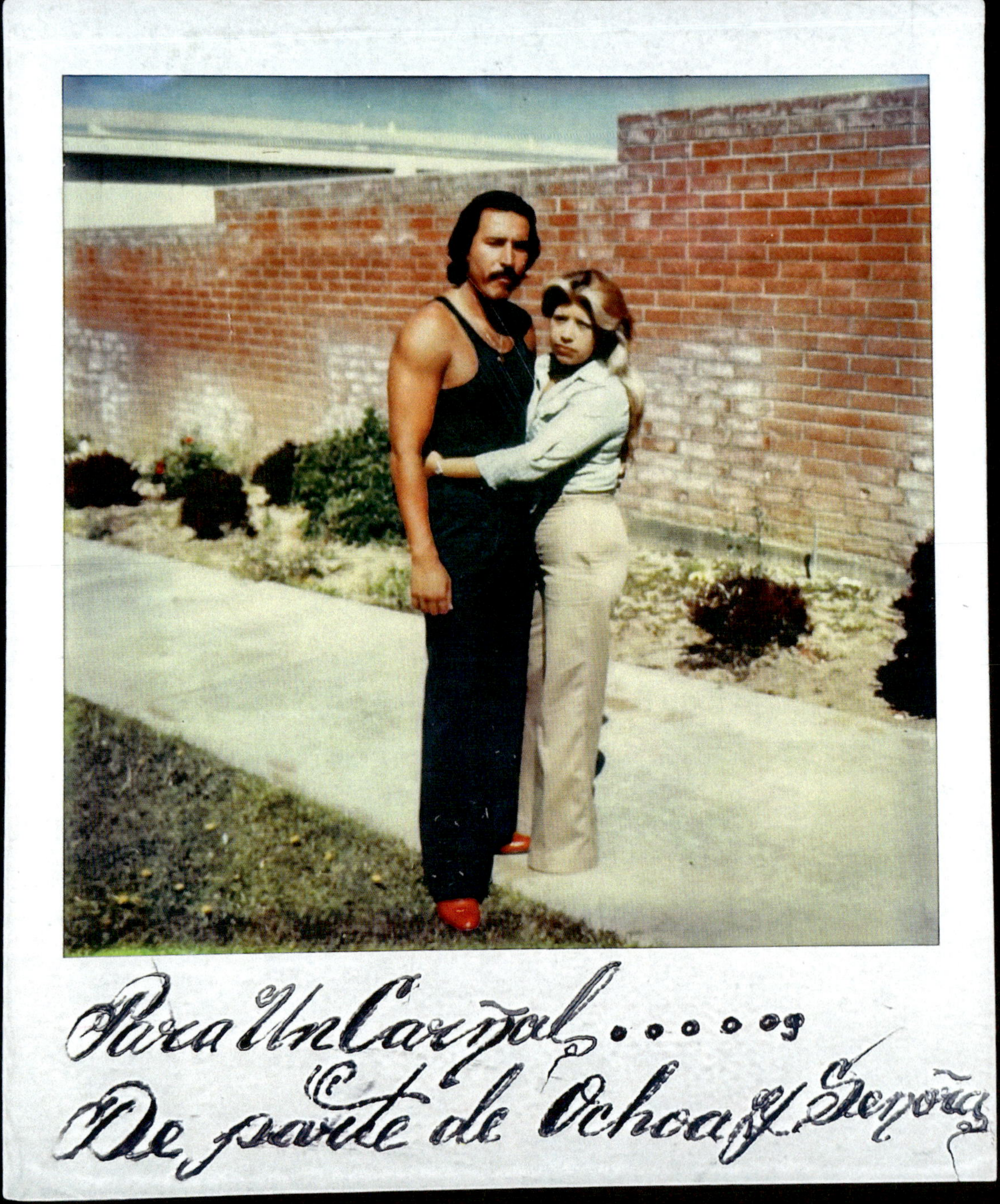


This photo was taken at Tehachapi Prison in 1978. This photo was part of Dangerous Dan DeAvila's collection.

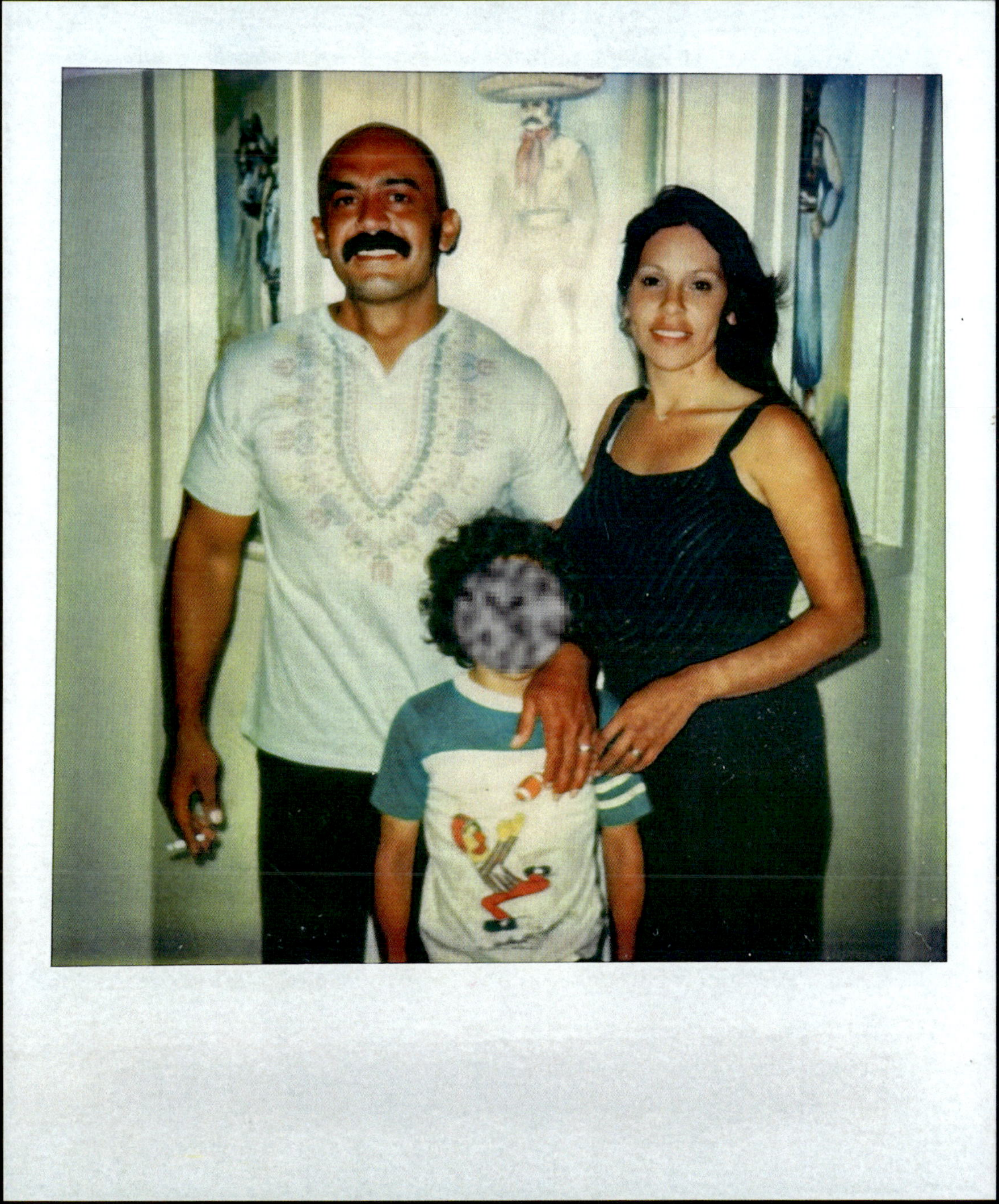

This photo was taken on July 4, 1978 at Tehachapi Prison during a visit.

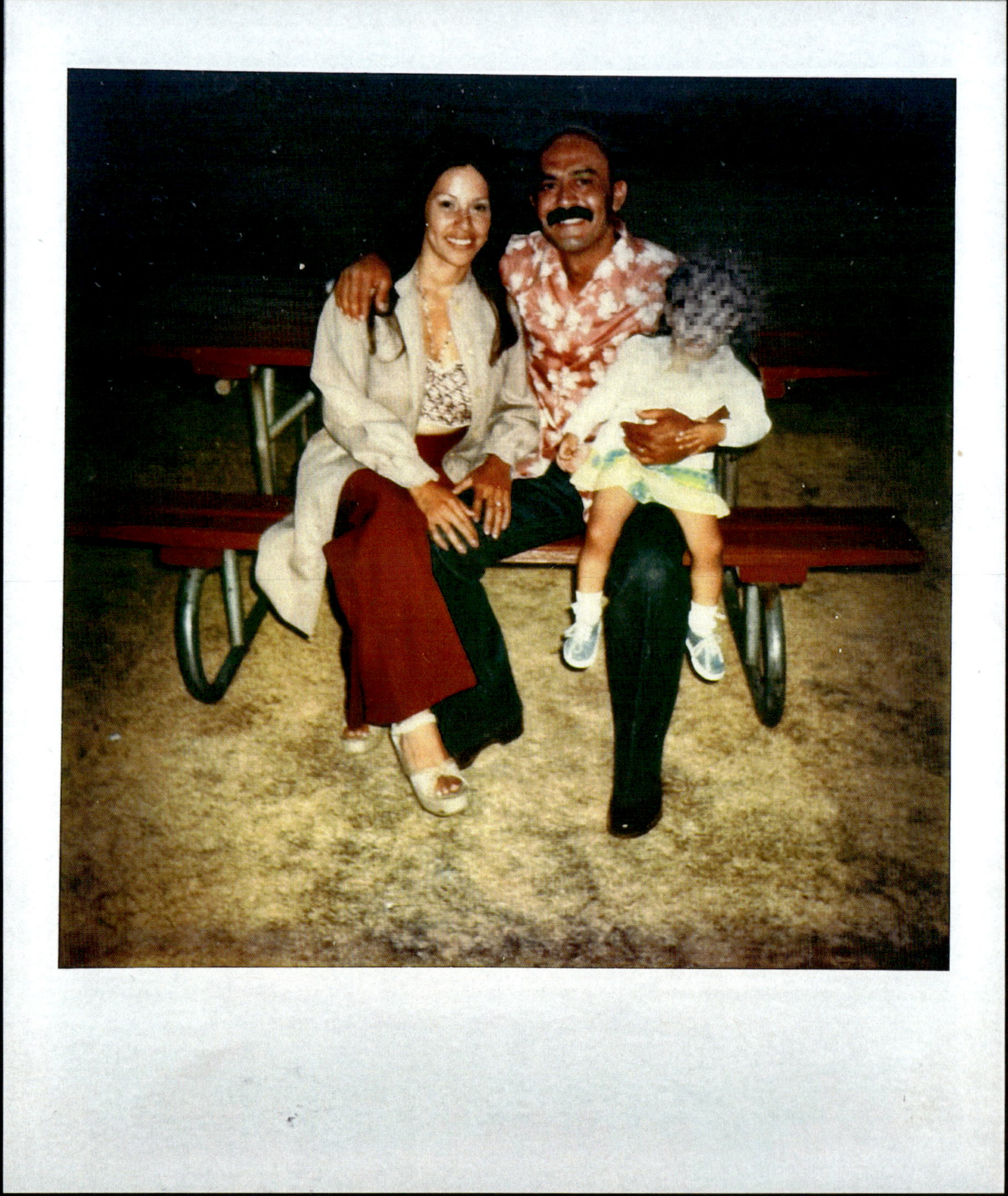

This photo was taken on June 21, 1978 at Tehachapi Prison during a visit.

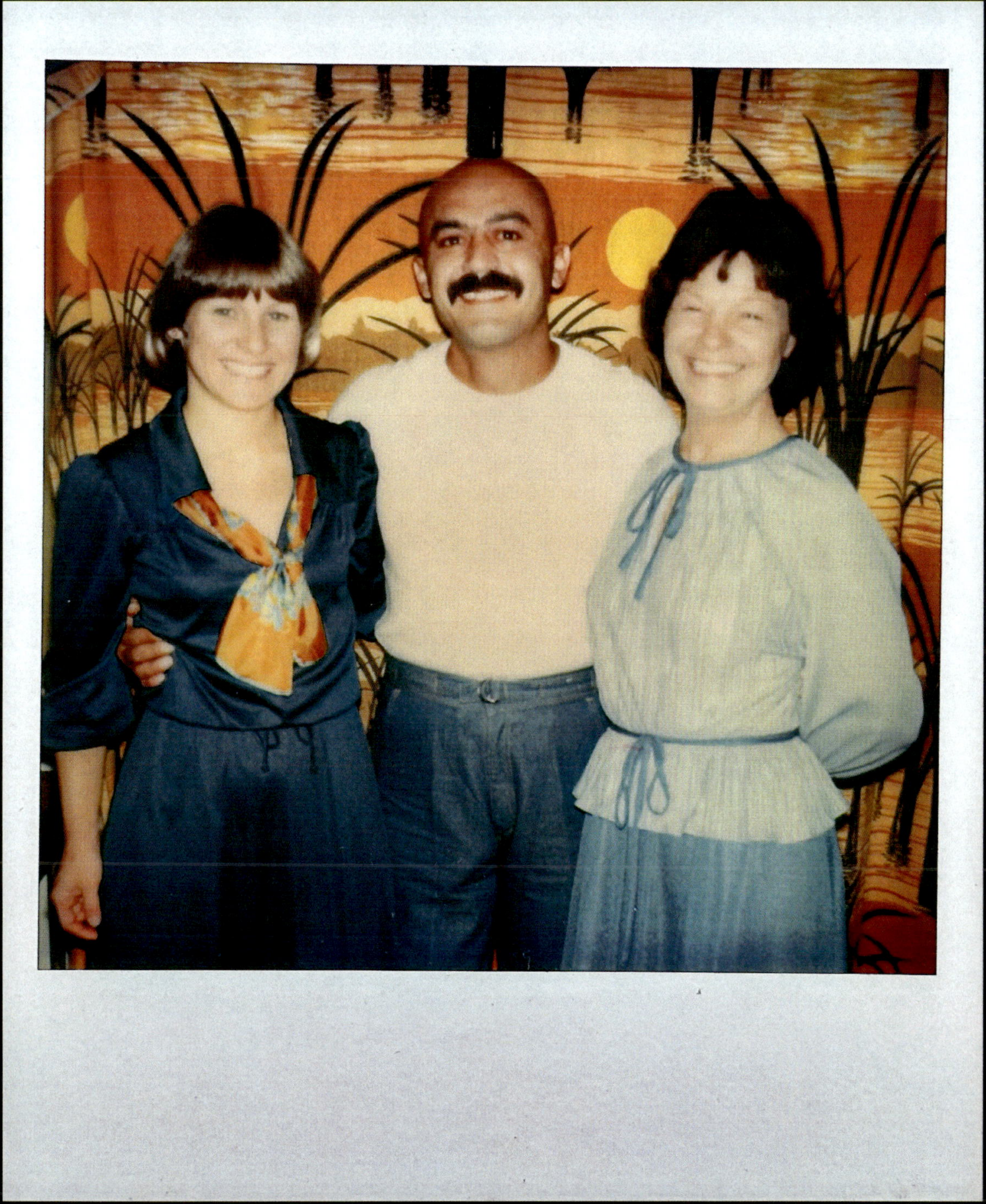

This photo was taken on January 5, 1979 at Tehachapi Prison during a visit.

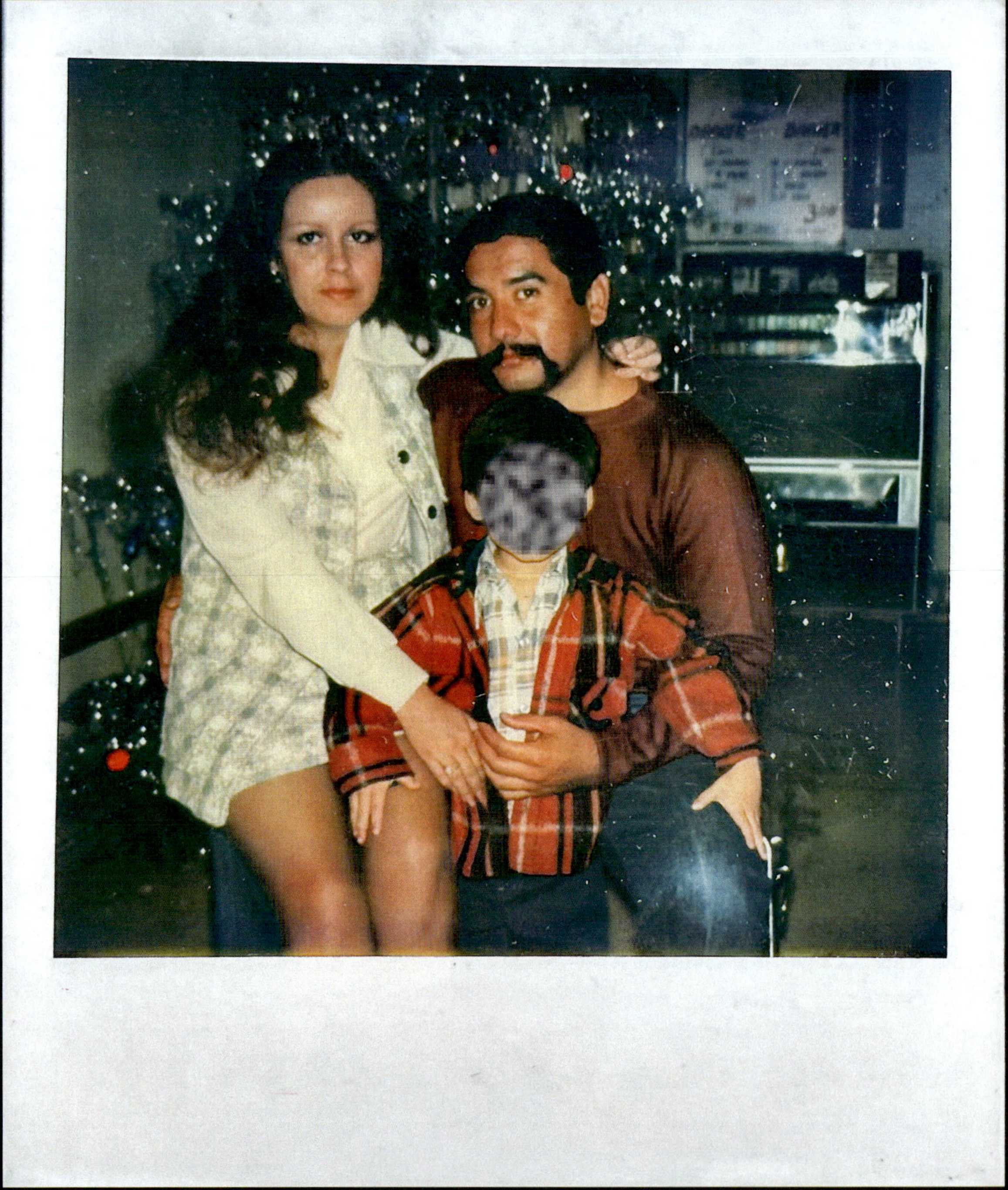

This photo was taken at Tehachapi Prison on December 26, 1978. This photo was part of Dangerous Dan DeAvila's collection.

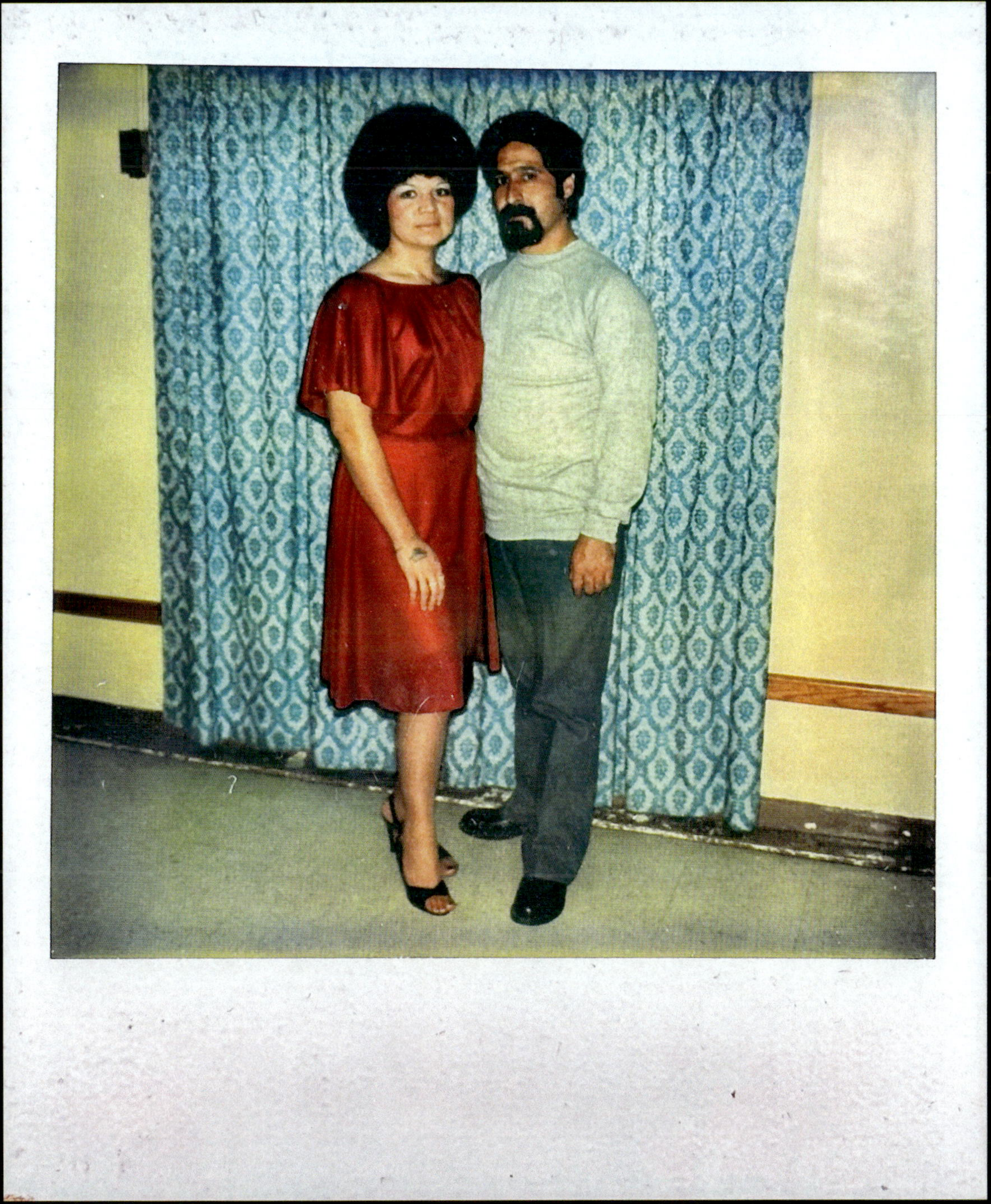

This photo was taken at Tehachapi Prison on March 7, 1980. This photo was part of Dangerous Dan DeAvila's collection.

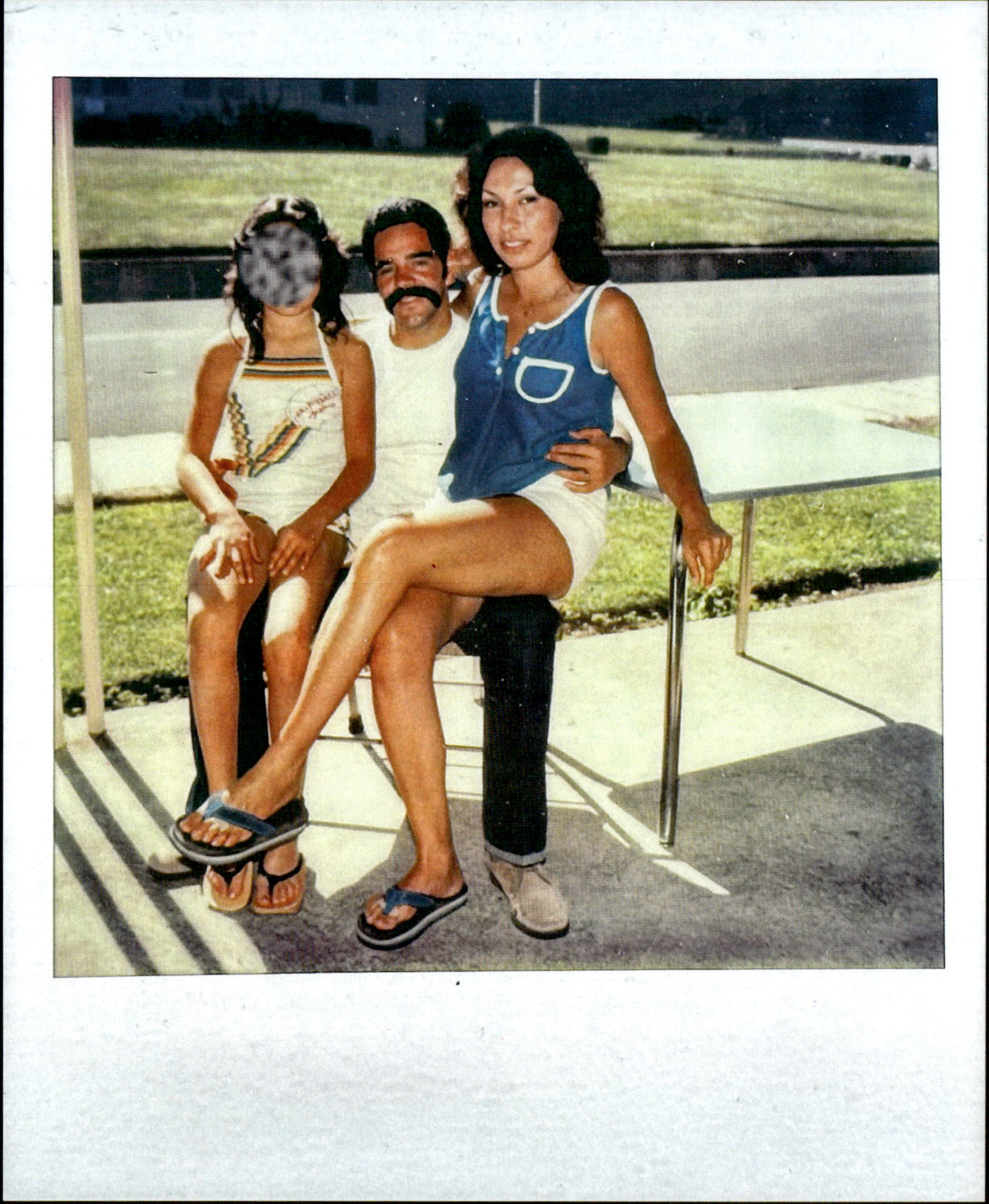

This photo was taken at Tehachapi Prison on June 27, 1979. This photo was part of Dangerous Dan DeAvila's collection.

# About the Author

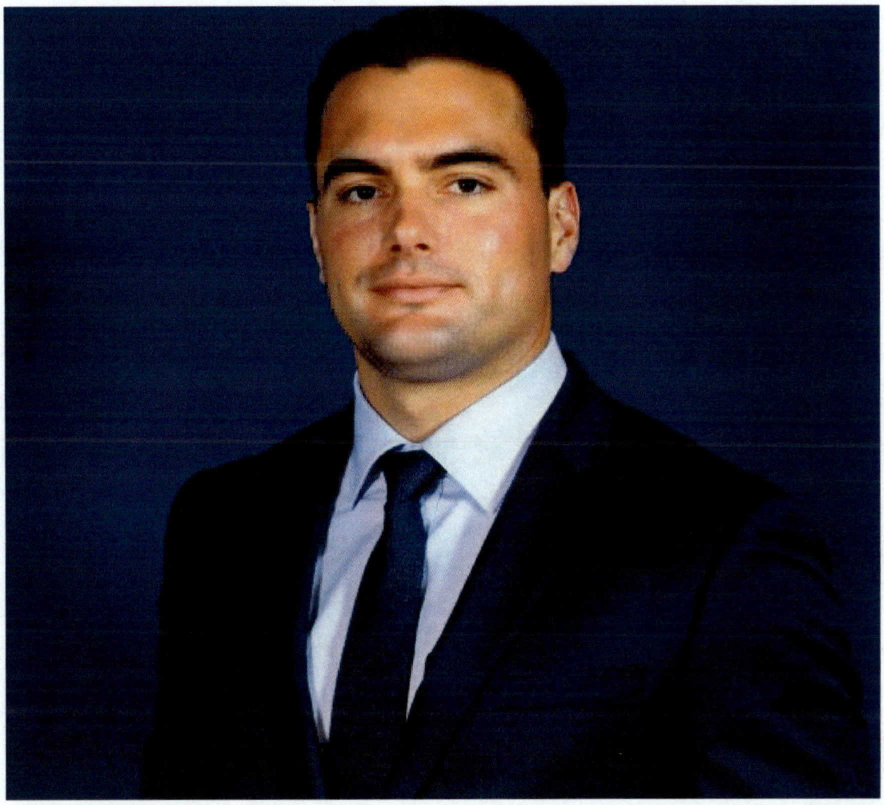

Eric has emerged as a highly accomplished investor and Day Trader, engaging in trading activities with a substantial value of stocks annually. He enjoys the status of a dedicated husband and father, being blessed with four wonderful daughters who hold a special place in his heart. Eric's existence revolves around upholding the virtues of a devout Christian, a devoted husband, and a caring father guided by the grace of God. His journey has been transformative, considering his challenging upbringing, and he now stands as an illustrious testament to the boundless possibilities achievable through faith in God.

Eric joined a criminal street gang as a teenager, and he was eventually arrested and put in a cage at the Long Beach City Jail. He dropped out of Jordan High School in Long Beach, California, in the 10th grade. Eric eventually got on the right path by the grace of God and obtained his GED the same month that he would have graduated. He joined the United States Coast Guard at 18, and after four years of faithful service, he was honorably discharged.

The following is an excerpt from his autobiography: "California Prison Confessions." "It was a typical beautiful summer night in Long Beach, California, and the three young teens fighting in the musty garage starkly contrasted the night's serenity. A teen called Bones was thrown against a wall, and a muscular teenager nicknamed E Double (me) rushed towards him and violently punched him in his lower back. Another youth named Tim Loc held Bones against the wall during this attack. E Double's knuckles landed with a thick-sounding thud as Bones grimaced and moaned in pain from each successive blow.

There's a look of pain and fear in Bone's eyes as E Double mercilessly lands blow after blow to his kidneys. E Double has spent years hitting the heavy bag in his garage, so his punches are devastating for his age. The beating lasted a minute, and the two teens stopped attacking the unfortunate victim. Amazingly, they all shook hands and embraced each other. We were all friends, and this was our modest gang initiation into our small clique called 'Six Feet Under.'"

Our tiny neighborhood gang in North Long Beach, California, had several members of various races: White, Black, and Hispanic. The definition of a criminal street gang according to the California Penal Code is as follows: "As used in this chapter, 'criminal street gang' means any ongoing organization, association, or group of three or more persons, whether formal or informal, having as one of its primary activities the commission of one or more of the criminal acts…having a common name or common identifying sign or symbol, and whose members individually or collectively engage in or have engaged in a pattern of criminal gang activity," California Penal Code 186.22(f).

Some of our associates committed serious crimes such as burglaries, drug sales, stealing cars, carrying guns, vandalism, and assaulting people. Although we were nothing but young punks, we were a criminal street gang according to the California Penal Code.

The FBI did a study entitled "Street-Gang Mentality: A Mosaic of Remorseless Violence and Relentless Loyalty." I want to quote a relevant part concerning young males who do not have a father or other positive male role models in their lives while growing up: "All gang members lacked male role models in their households, and when they lived with their mothers, they were rarely home because of work schedules. Gang members often lived temporarily with various people. All but one gang member reported that one or more immediate family members had a criminal history or abused drugs. Gangs attracted them because of their loyalty, stability, and sense of group identity."

There is an epidemic in this country of boys masquerading as men who don't take their responsibilities as fathers seriously. Many fathers aren't involved in their children's lives; if they are, they are a horrible example of what a real man should be. One of the main factors in young men ending up in the penal system is the lack of a father or, at the very least, a positive male role model when they were growing up. Absentee fathers are causing society to pay a high price for their selfish and callous actions.

Every day, I strive to be the best dad to the four beautiful daughters God has blessed me with. I live by the motto, "Be the man you needed as a child." I will not allow the actions of physically and emotionally abusive people to define who I am or hinder my advancement in life. You can choose to be bitter or better. I strive for excellence because living well is the best response to abusive people.

Eric Sturgess

God bless you and yours.

Romans 10:9-13

For those seeking to connect with Eric or gather additional insights about his upcoming projects, please visit his official website: EricSturgess.com.

# Other Books

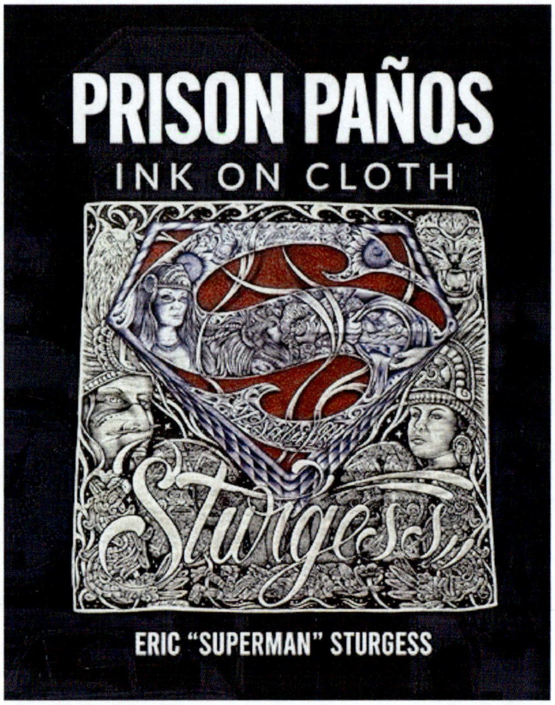


Prison Paños: Ink On Cloth

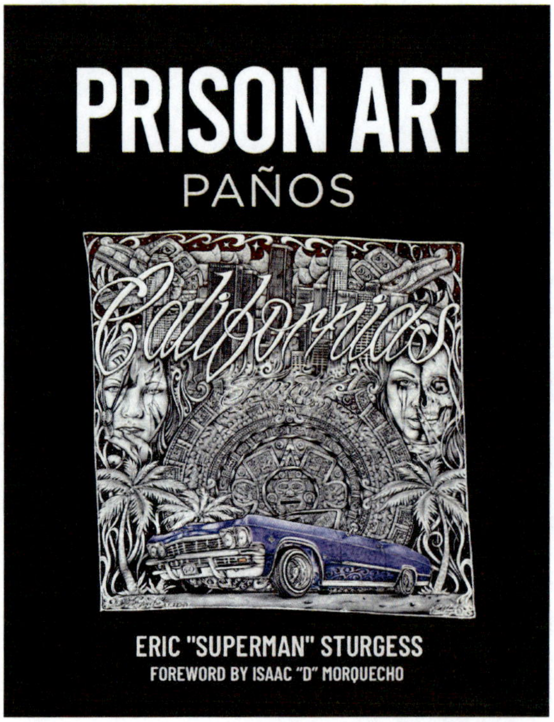


Prison Art Paños

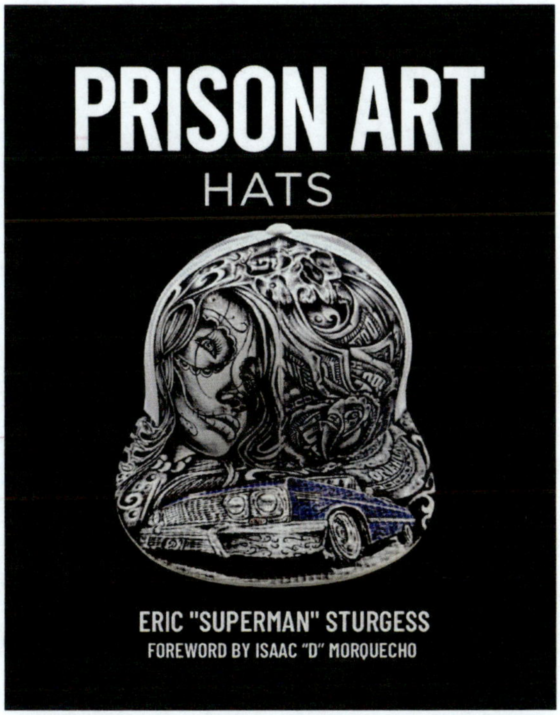


Prison Art Hats

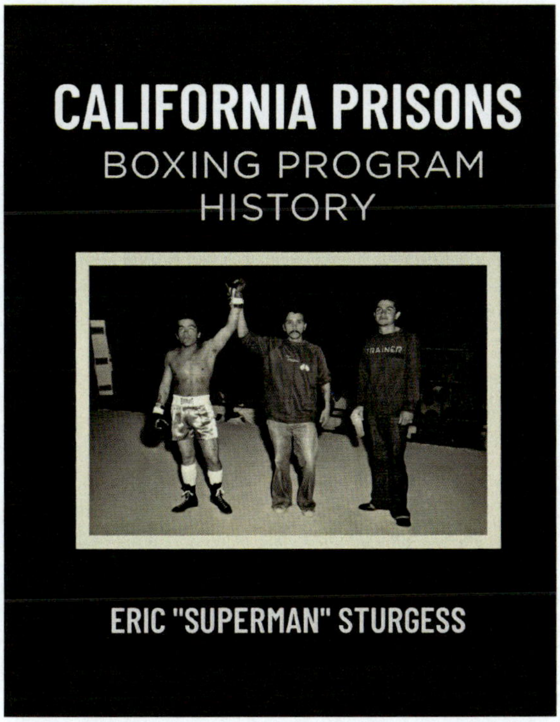


California Prisons:
Boxing Program History

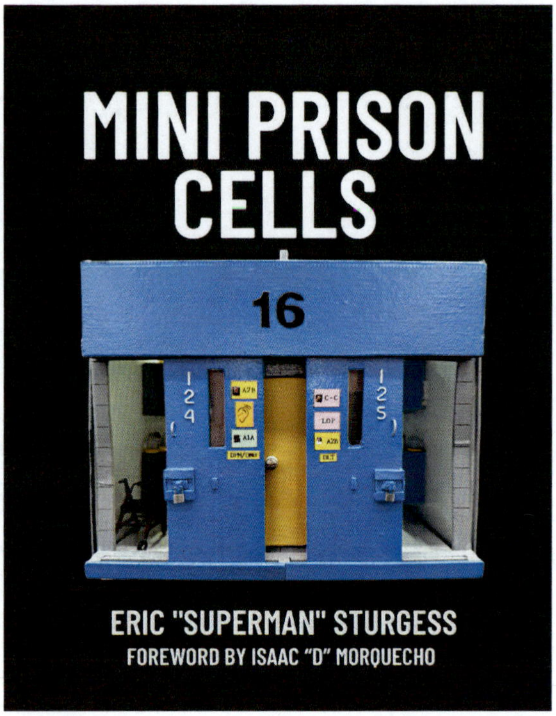


Mini Prison Cells

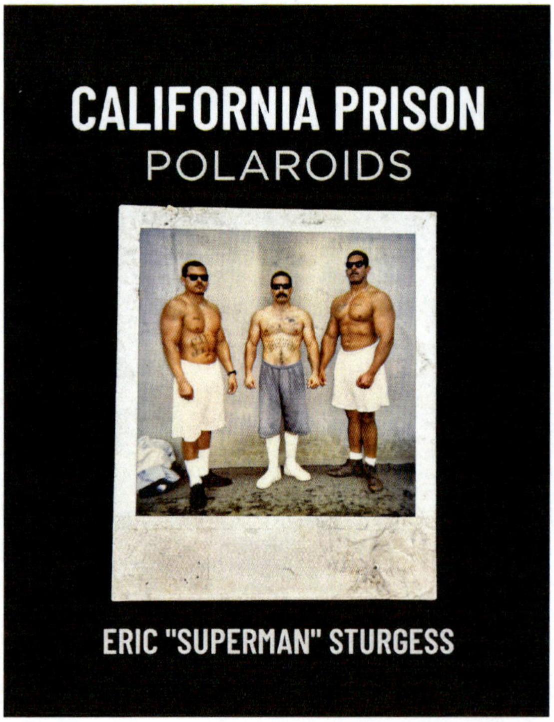


California Prison Polaroids

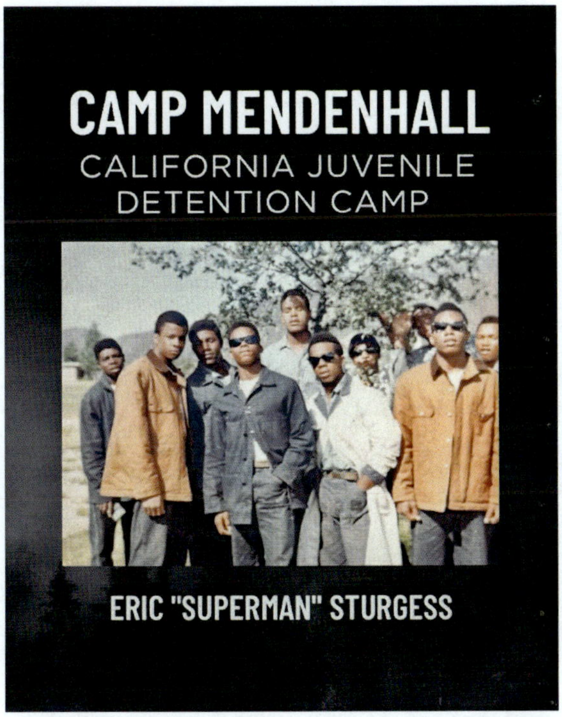


Camp Mendenhall: California Juvenile Detention Camp

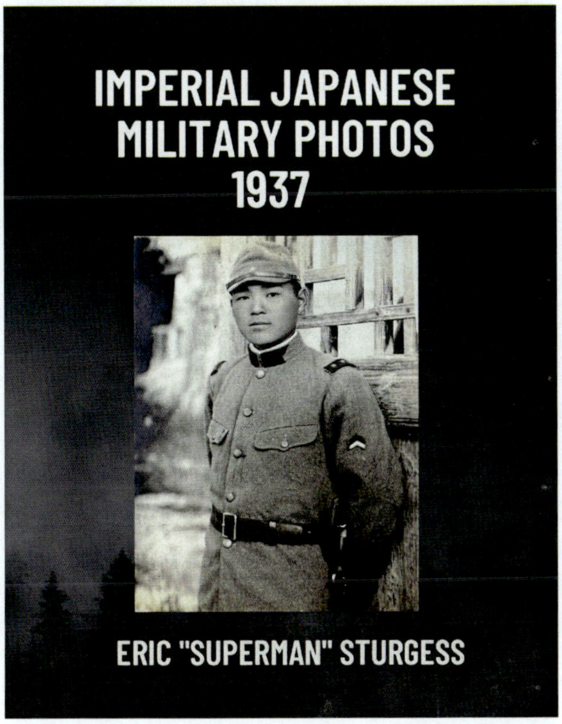


Imperial Japanese Military Photos 1937

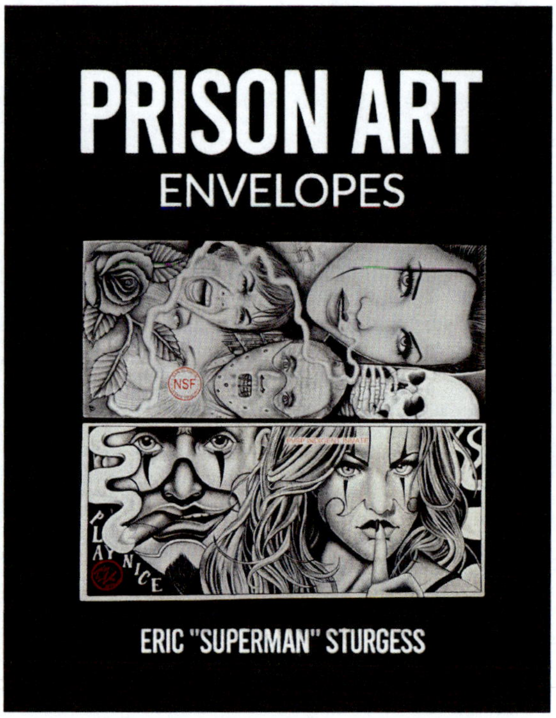


Prison Art Envelopes

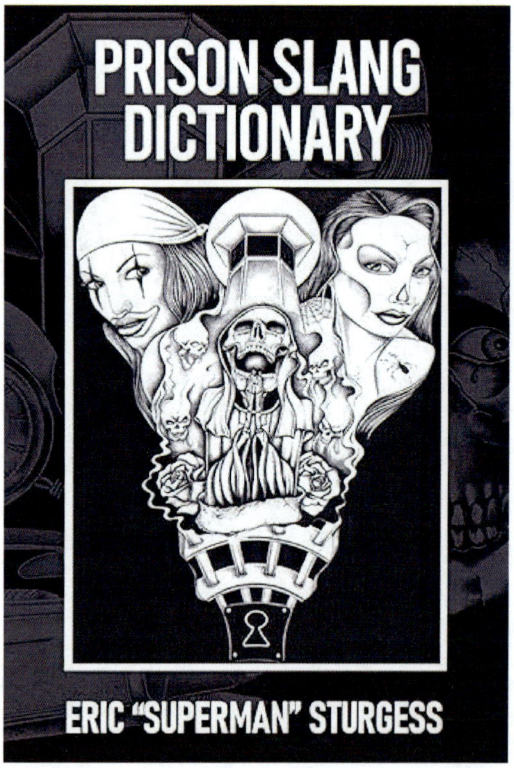


Prison Slang Dictionary

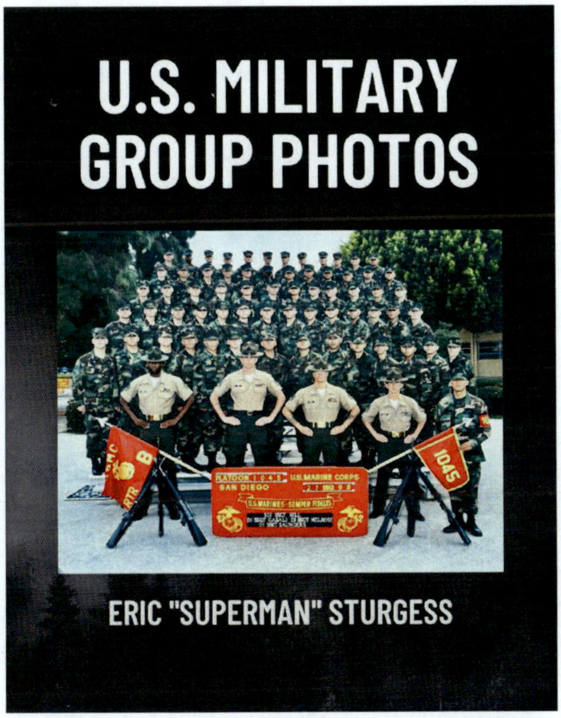


U.S. Military Group Photos

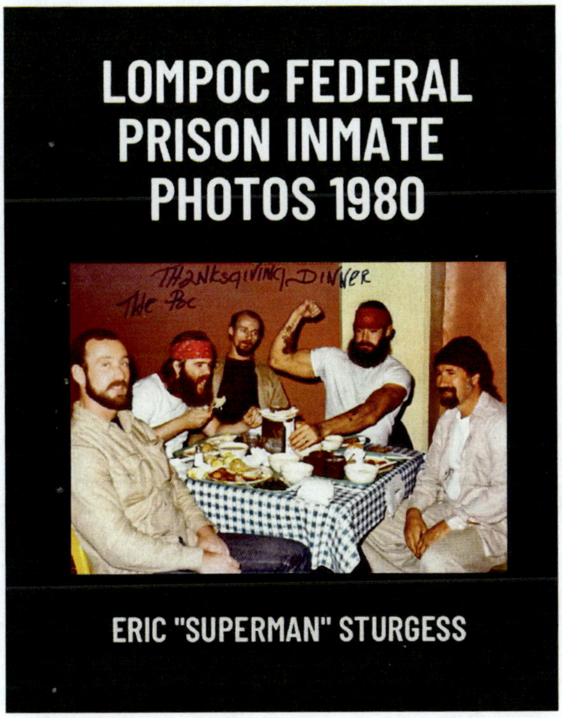


Lompoc Federal Prison Inmate Photos 1980

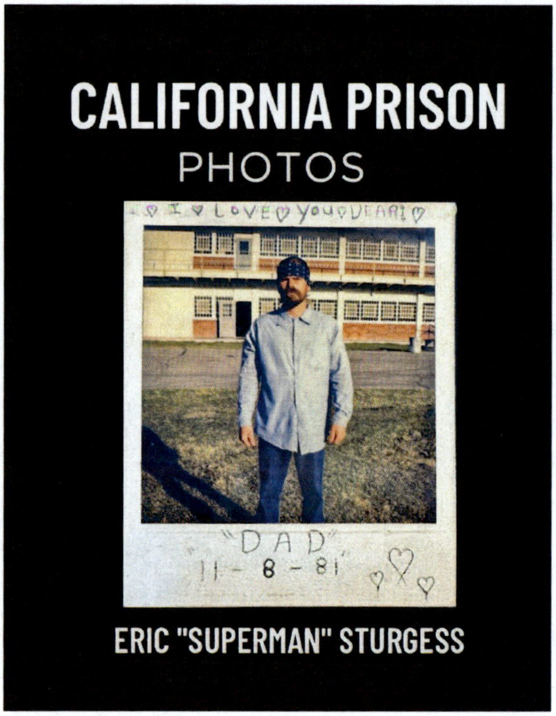


California Prison Photos

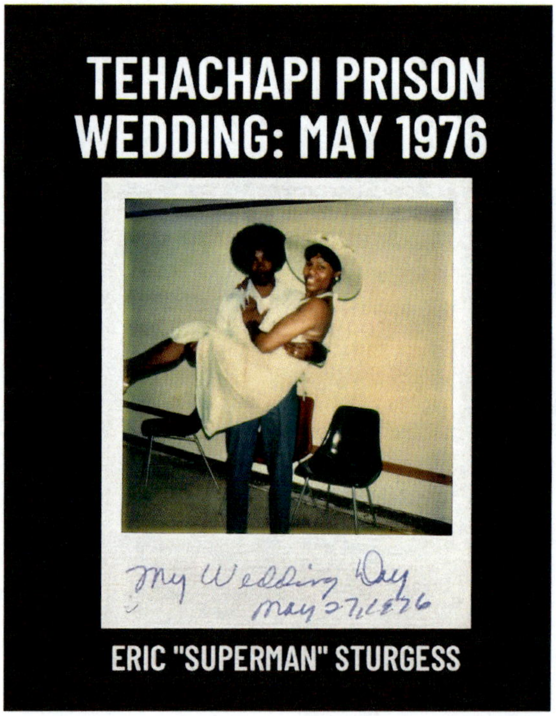


Tehachapi Prison Wedding: May 1976

Made in United States
North Haven, CT
05 November 2026

21765029R00022